Mountains are enormous bits of rock that stand much higher than the ground around them. Some are on their own, while others are part of a chain.

They can be many different shapes with rounded tops or jagged peaks. It all depends on how the mountains were formed and how old they are.

1

The top layer of the Earth is called the crust. This crust is made up of several big chunks. These chunks are called "tectonic plates", and they are not fixed in one spot.

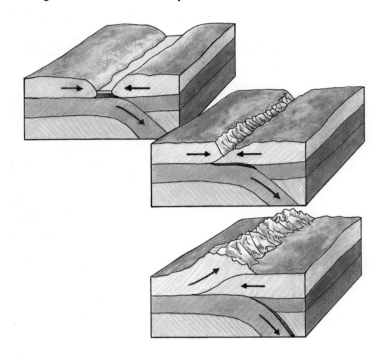

The sides of these plates hit against each other. When this happens, the layers of rock in the Earth's crust are folded up to form mountains.

Many mountains are still growing, while some are getting smaller. As soon as a mountain has formed, it starts to be worn away by the weather. Wind, rain, frost, streams and rivers attack the rock. Slowly, the mountain gets smaller and becomes less jagged.

The Himalayan Mountains stretch across four countries. The three highest mountains in the Himalayas are Mount Everest, K2, and Kangchenjunga.

The mountains here are so tall because they are quite young and have not been worn down yet.

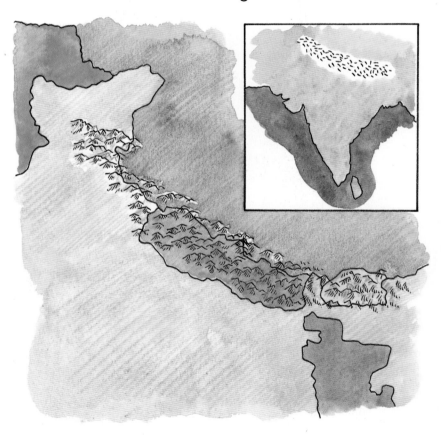

The highest mountain is Mount Everest. Many mountaineers have died trying to reach the top of it. Sir Edmund Hilary and Sherpa Tensing Norgay were the first men to reach the top on May 29, 1953.

A high mountain has different zones at its top, middle and bottom. Trees grow in the lowest zone at the bottom of the mountain. They cannot grow higher up.

The part around the mountainside where the trees stop growing is called the tree line.

At the top of a mountain is a zone where there is snow all the time. It is very cold and very difficult to survive here.

The part around the mountainside where the zone begins is called the snow line. In Antarctica, the snow line is at the bottom of the mountain!

Some flowers can grow between the tree line and the snow line of a mountain. Flowers that grow here are called "alpines". They tend to be small and keep out of the wind. They have long roots to help them grip and hold on to the mountainside.

Many animals have adapted so that they can live in the mountains. Sheep and goats can live high up on steep, rocky mountainsides. They have rubbery pads on their hooves to help them on the slopes.

Many animals that live in the mountains have thick fur coats to keep out the cold. A yak is a sort of cow that lives in the Himalayas, mainly in Tibet. The Tibetans use the yaks for meat, milk, clothes and tents. The yaks carry the tents, food and packs across the mountains.

The Rocky Mountains run down from northern Canada to the southern USA. They are sometimes called "America's backbone". When the settlers were going across America, they found the Rocky Mountains very difficult to cross.

The Matterhorn is a mountain in Switzerland. It is easy to recognise because of its shape. The chain of mountains that runs across Switzerland is called the Alps.

In the Alps, farmers live in the valleys between the mountains and grow crops there in the summer.

Also in the summer, they send their cows up the mountainsides to graze. In the winter, they bring the cows back down into the valleys.

The milk from cows is used to make cheese and chocolate. Swiss cheese and chocolate are very well known.

A long time ago, Saint Bernard lived in the mountains between Switzerland and Italy. He set up a hostel where anyone could rest as they went across the mountains. He gave them free food and shelter. Sometimes, they would get lost in the snow.

Saint Bernard trained some dogs to help him go out and rescue those who had got lost. The dogs were big and had thick fur coats. They were strong and could dig out anyone who had got trapped in the snow.

Little barrels were hung from the dogs' collars. Inside the barrels was something to drink for those who had been lost or trapped.

The dogs were so big that they could help those they had rescued back to the hostel and safety. This sort of dog is still called a Saint Bernard today.